MY LIFE AND TIMES

By Shirley Temple

As Told to Max Trell

Copyright MCMXXXVI

THE SAALFIELD PUBLISHING COMPANY

AKRON, OHIO NEW YORK

Publishers for the Children

Made in U. S. A.
Registered at Stationers' Hall

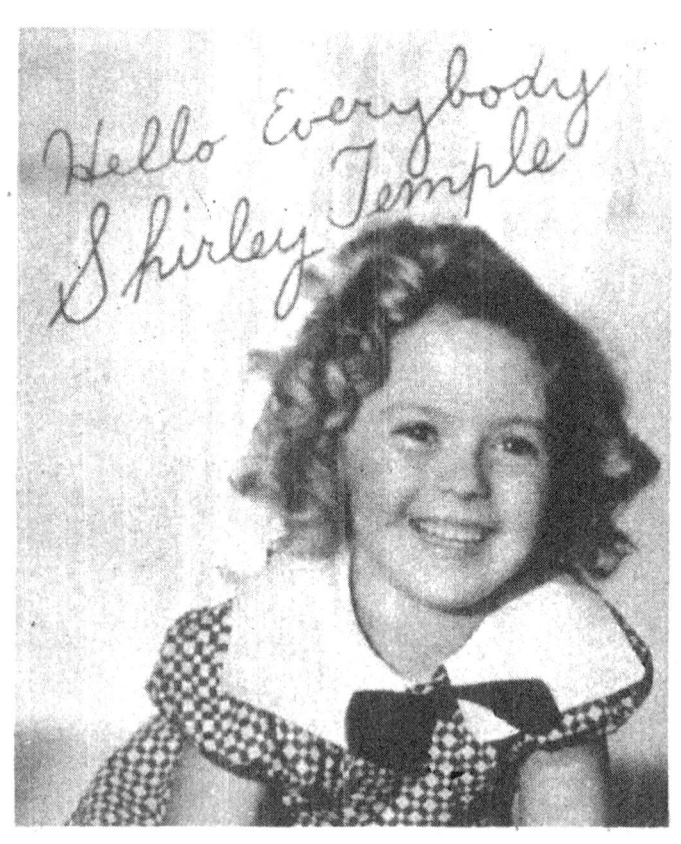

Now sit up, Corky.

MY LIFE AND TIMES

The Autobiography of Shirley Temple

NOW sit up, Corky. I'm going to tell you a story. It's all going to be about me. Well, some of it will be about you, but only a little bit because you're only a little Scotty.

Mom and Daddy, and Jack and Sonny—they're my big brothers (and I haven't got any little ones)—are going to be in the story, too. And so are the five rabbits, and the two turtles with the painted backs, and the cocker spaniel Rowdy, and all the dolls from Italy and France and London and New York and

MY LIFE AND TIMES

Japan and Hawaii, and Janet Gaynor, and Mr. Winfield Sheehan, and my teacher Miss Barkley, and Jimmy Dunn (whom I like best of all right now), and Gary Cooper, and poor Mr. Will Rogers who was killed last year, and Jack Donohue, and—well, you just keep your ears up and listen. You're only one year old. You're just a puppy. You hardly know anything yet. I'm six years old. I'm grown up.

The story begins way back in 1929. That's the year when I was born, Corky. Mom and Daddy and especially the friends down at Daddy's bank in Los Angeles—he's the manager of the bank—always called me Shirley, the Depression Baby, because I was born in the year of the crash.

Shirley, the Depression Baby.
One year old.

MY LIFE AND TIMES

I don't know what the crash was but I guess it was something lucky for me, and lucky for the rest of the Temple family. Great big Mr. Irvin Cobb with the red face, who gave me the statuette of myself at the Motion Picture Academy banquet last year, said that when Santa Claus dropped me down the chimney of the world it was a lucky day for millions of people everywhere. So I don't suppose Shirley, the Depression Baby, was anything so very bad.

It's a pity you never saw the house where we used to live. It wasn't nearly so big as the house we're living in now. It only had five little rooms and a garden. My bed was in the same room with Daddy and Mom. Now I have my own room, and a room just for my

MY LIFE AND TIMES

dolls. Daddy and Mom have their own room, and so have the two boys (except that Sonny goes to military academy now in New Mexico and doesn't use his room). Why, there's even a room downstairs where my secretary, Miss Dorothy Drum, opens my fan letters and sends out stills of me in different pictures. And there's a big kitchen, and a dining room, and a beautiful patio.

Oh, the patio's a fine place, Corky! It's where I play. It's like a lovely cool garden inside your own house. There's a goldfish pool in the middle of it, and a banana tree with real bananas growing on it, and different kinds of cactus standing in little spaces along the sides. I can't roll around on the grass because there isn't any grass. The floor

Don't you think I look like my mother?

Mom was four years old when this was taken.

MY LIFE AND TIMES

is covered with brown tiles. But nobody can see me from the street when I play in the patio. And that's the best thing of all.

You know, when you're a movie star, Corky, people always want to see what you look like. And they touch you, and shake your hand, and pat you on the head, and ask you how you're feeling, and will you please write your name on a piece of paper for them. And sometimes they suddenly put their arms around you and kiss you!

So you see, Corky, it's a good thing that I play in a closed-in patio now instead of the open garden that we used to have. I remember the fun it was when I first got my bicycle. Brother Jack—he's twenty-one now and he's six-foot-two—he said it wasn't a bicycle

MY LIFE AND TIMES

at all but a tricycle because it had three wheels. But it was great sport riding up and down and all around the narrow paths in our old garden. The paths were just wide enough for the wheels. If I went too fast I tumbled into Mom's flower beds, or ran into the washline.

Once I went on a long trip without even leaving the garden. I went to Erie, Pennsylvania. That is where Daddy lived when he was a little boy. I pretended it was down by the eucalyptus trees at the end of the garden. The next day I went all the way to Chicago. That's Mom's home town. But Daddy and Mom came to California when they were pretty young. They first met here. They got married here. Jack and Sonny (and Sonny

Once I went on a long trip.

MY LIFE AND TIMES

isn't his real name; it's George, Jr., after Daddy) were born here. So was I. I'm a real Californian.

The nicest thing in the old garden was my wooden playhouse. I can't remember when it was given to me. I must have been less than three years old. You don't remember many things when you're that small, Corky—I mean, little children don't. It was a bigger place than the new doghouse which the carpenters on the Fox lot have built for you and Rowdy. I could stand up in it, and it had a door and a window. One day Mom bought me a little table and chair—my first furniture. I still have them, only I don't use them any more. They've been put away somewhere. The little playhouse is gone, too.

MY LIFE AND TIMES

Now I have a bungalow at the studio. That's my real playhouse today. It's got small furniture in it, too. And a small dressing room, and even a small bathroom!

Some of the chairs are so narrow that Mr. David Butler—he directed me and Mr. Lionel Barrymore and Mr. Bill Robinson and Evelyn Venable and all the others in *The Little Colonel*—can't even squeeze himself into them. I'm glad that he can't. He'd most likely find himself sitting on the floor the next minute, and I'd find myself with a broken chair. Mr. Butler weighs about a ton, I guess. He's the fattest man I know. One day while we were resting for a few minutes on the set of *Bright Eyes*—he directed that one, too—he called me over and

Jolly Mr. David Butler directed "The Littlest Rebel,"
my newest picture.

MY LIFE AND TIMES

said, "Come here, Shirley, and sit on my lap." That made me laugh. "You can't fool me, Mr. Butler," I said to him. "Asking me to sit on your lap! Why, you haven't even got a lap."

That little table and chair from my wooden playhouse in the garden came in handy lots of times, Corky. You see, our old house was in Santa Monica. That's a town right next to Beverly Hills and Hollywood. You'd almost think from looking at them that they were all one town because all the streets and houses run together. You've got to be kind of smart to be able to tell where one of them ends and the next one begins. There's one thing about Santa Monica, though, that's different from the other two. It's nearest the

The nicest thing in the old garden
was my wooden playhouse.

MY LIFE AND TIMES

beach and that's where the Pacific Ocean is!

We could walk down to the beach from our old house. We can walk to it from our new house, too. We still live in Santa Monica, you know, not very far from where we used to live, only in a different neighborhood. The quickest way to get to the beach is to get into Mom's new car. But we don't go to the beach any more. I'm too busy at the studio. If I'm not making a picture, I'm going to school—oh, not really going to school, just studying reading and writing and French with Miss Barkley in my bungalow on the lot. I'll tell you more about all that later.

But I don't think we would go to the same old beach even if I did have time. Too many people would come crowding around me.

MY LIFE AND TIMES

Why, one summer we went to Balboa—that's a beach a little distance away from Los Angeles. We stayed there about two weeks while Daddy was on his vacation from the bank. I was having a fine time on the sand with the children. I told them my name was Shirley, and they told me their names. Then one morning a lady stopped in front of me and said, "My goodness, you look just like Shirley Temple!"

I thought that was very funny. So I laughed and said, "That's who I am—Shirley Temple."

She didn't know whether to believe me or not for a minute or two. She came over and looked at me closer. Then she saw Daddy and Mom sitting near by, and she got so excited she didn't know what to say. But finally she begged them to let me write my name for her in a little book which she took out of her purse. So Mom called me, and I had to stop digging the tunnel with the other children and start writing my name in her book. I couldn't write very well that summer. I really couldn't write at all. I could only print: *LOVE—SHIRLEY TEMPLE*. And that took a long time to do. But I did it. The lady thanked me a lot when I finished and smiled and told me that she had a little niece just my size back East who would be very glad to know that she had spoken to the real Shirley Temple.

Then she left, and I went back to digging the tunnel. But pretty soon more people be-

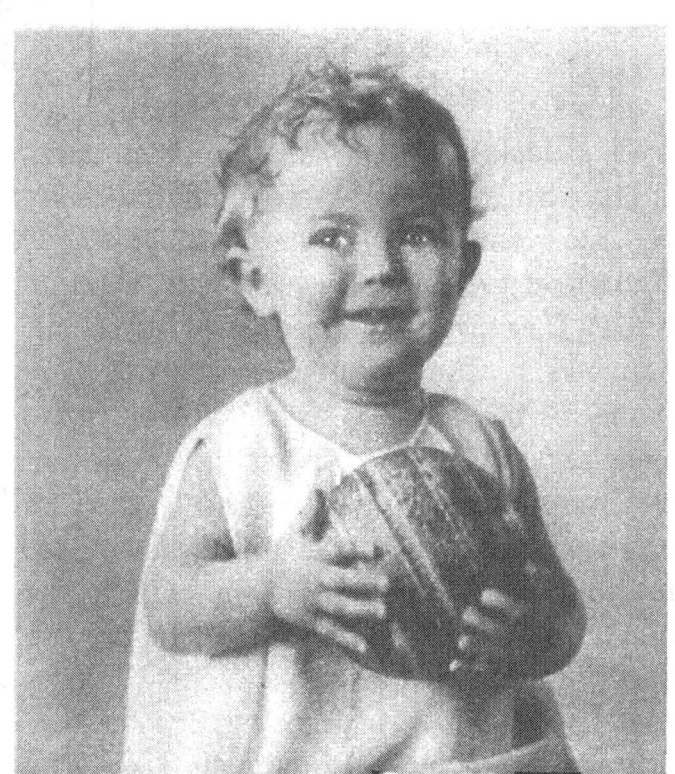

I was just a baby here, only eighteen months old!

MY LIFE AND TIMES

gan coming over. Some of them just passed by and looked at me. Some of them said, "Hello, Shirley!" I answered hello. I really felt like saying, "Please don't bother me now. Can't you see how busy I am with this tunnel?" But they bent over me with pencils and books. They wanted me to print my name for them, too. Then Mom went up to them and explained in a very nice voice that she was sorry that I wouldn't be able to give any more autographs because it was time for me to take my nap. We went back to the hotel. It wasn't time for me to take my nap at all. Daddy sat me on his knees. "I guess that's what you get for being famous, darling," he said. He read me a story out of a book.

This is another baby picture. Here I'm two.

MY LIFE AND TIMES

I kept glancing out of the window. I couldn't help thinking it would have been more fun just digging in the sand.

Mom and Daddy always took my little table and chair down to the beach in Santa Monica when I was very small. Can you guess the reason why, Corky? I'll tell you. I used to eat my lunch on my own table, right out in the sunshine. Mom brought soup, or cereal, or vegetables—all warm—in a big thermos jug. She always said she thought it was a good idea for me to keep having my regular hot meals even though we were away from home. Do you know that even when I first started acting for the movies (I was only about three and a half years old then) Mom took that same thermos jug to the studio with

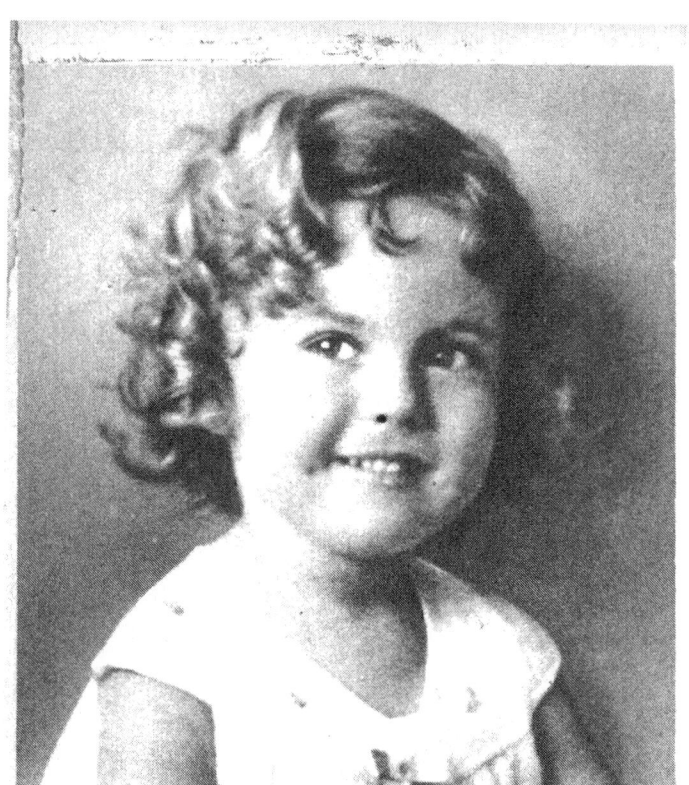

I was just three years old then, so all those things happened in the middle of my life.

MY LIFE AND TIMES

us? The other women would sometimes laugh at Mom and say she was being too particular about my diet, but she kept right on bringing it. "Studio or no studio," she said, "my Presh"—she really meant Precious—"my Presh is going to eat properly."

I always liked to dance. That's what Mom says. She must be right because she knows me better than anyone else. I've heard her say that she could tell I liked to dance as soon as I began to walk. I didn't walk like other children, she said. I seemed to skip along like a fairy-child. And whenever she turned on the radio in our house and I heard the music, I danced the prettiest steps of all.

I'll tell you a secret, Corky. Lots of times it wasn't Mom at all who turned on the radio.

MY LIFE AND TIMES

I turned it on myself. Round and round the living room I danced. I made up my own steps as I went along. I don't dance much by myself any more. And I don't make up my own steps much, either. I've got enough to do learning the steps that Mr. Jack Donohue, who teaches me dancing at the studio, makes up for me for my different pictures. Mr. Bill Robinson—you remember the stair dance I did with him in *The Little Colonel?*—he says that when I get older I'll know enough to make up my own steps, like all good dancers do.

One night as Daddy was giving me my bath—I was about three then and I'm six now and Daddy still gives me my bath—Mom started to tell him that she thought it

The next morning Mom took me to dancing school.

MY LIFE AND TIMES

would be a nice idea to let me go to dancing school. She said that some of the other little children on the block were going. "It's only one class a week, George," I remember her saying, "and it costs only fifty cents."

Daddy didn't look very pleased. He said he thought I was pretty young to be going to dancing school. And anyhow he didn't want me to become a dancer. He said nobody in his family and nobody in Mom's family had ever been on the stage or in the films, and he didn't see what good my learning to dance would do any of us; and no, he couldn't see it.

Mom smiled and said it wasn't anything so serious. It's true we lived near the Hollywood film studios, she went on. But what did they have to do with us, or we with them?

MY LIFE AND TIMES

"We might just as well be living in Chicago or Erie for all the movies mean in our lives," she said. "It will be lots of fun for Shirley to dance with the other children, George. That's all I'm thinking of. Of course, if the movies come after her with a big fat contract—well, that will be different!" She and Daddy laughed at that.

The next morning Mom took me to dancing school. It wasn't far from our house. I wore my best dress. But when we got there the teacher said that the next time I came it would be better just to give me a plain old dress. All the other little girls in the dancing class were wearing plain dresses. The boys were wearing little suits. Mom sat down on a long bench along the wall with the other

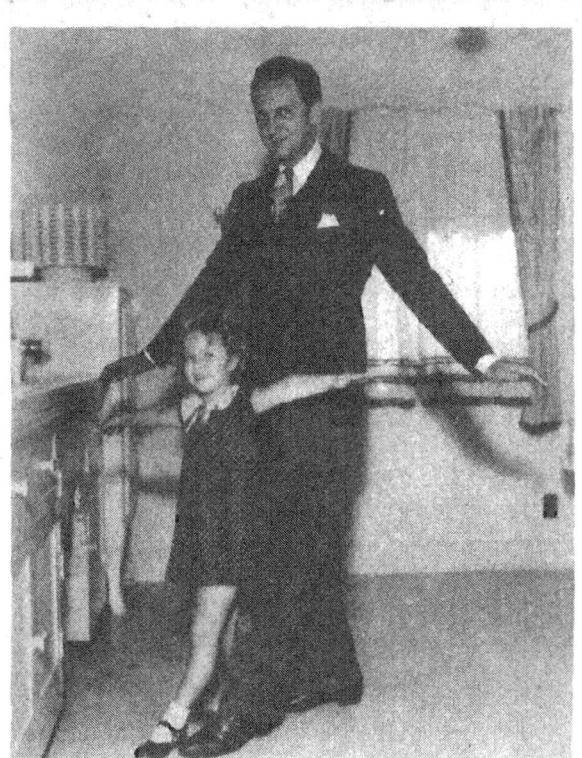

I have my dancing lessons in my bungalow kitchen.

MY LIFE AND TIMES

mothers. They kept watching us all through the lesson. The teacher made us stand in line. Then she did a little jumping step, and we all had to do it after her, first on one foot, then on the other, while somebody played " 'Way Down Upon the Suwanee River" on the piano.

Oh, how mixed up my feet got, Corky! I'm glad you weren't there. You'd be ashamed of me, I know.

But I can't always make my feet do what I'd like them to do. The dances that look so easy when you see me do them on the screen take hours and hours of hard work. Even the little steps in *Stand Up and Cheer* and *Baby Take a Bow* were terribly hard to do at first. I didn't think I'd ever learn that dance

MY LIFE AND TIMES

with Mr. Robinson on the stairs. And it was the same thing all over again for me when I had to begin learning the new routine for my picture *Curly Top*. Only I work with all my might on my dances, and I always end by knowing them so well that I find it pretty hard ever to forget them again, even when I don't need them any more. Every time I meet Jimmy Dunn on the lot we always go into the little dance we first did in *Baby Take a Bow*. Then we shake hands and say hello. But I first did that Baby Bow dance two years ago when I was only four and a half years old. And I haven't forgotten it yet!

I worked very hard on that little jumping step after my first lesson in dancing school.

MY LIFE AND TIMES

I jumped all over our house and all over the garden. I kept bothering Jack and Sonny, who were going to school and wanted to study. I wanted them to watch me but they said, "Go away; don't be a pest, Shirley." I don't blame them now. The step wasn't very much to watch—just up and down and a little shake with my toes. But my two big brothers are proud of me now. Only the other day Jack came home from school—he's in Stanford University this year—with two of his friends and brought them upstairs to see me in my private doll room. He sounded very important when he said, "And that's my little sister Shirley, over there, sitting on the floor." Then, just to show them that I really was his sister, he bent over

Every time I meet Jimmy Dunn on the lot we go into the little dance we first did in "Baby Take a Bow."

MY LIFE AND TIMES

and kissed me. His two friends couldn't do *that*, no, sir! I hear that Sonny brags about me to his schoolmates at his military school in New Mexico. But he and Jack certainly didn't care much about my first dances.

Well, Corky, by about the fifth or sixth lesson my feet began to behave themselves. I could jump around pretty well and I could even do the beginning of a soft-shoe tap step. When I practiced at home I either turned on the radio or else I hummed to myself. I generally hummed "Suwanee River." After a while I began to sing that pretty well, too. I mean, you could tell I wasn't singing "Yankee Doodle" or "My Old Kentucky Home." Mom played the piano a little, a couple of fingers at a time, and I sang with

MY LIFE AND TIMES

her. That's how I practice my songs for my pictures even now. Mom taps out the notes on the piano and I sing them. Mr. Sheehan —he's the man who used to run the Fox studio—wanted me to take piano lessons. He gave me a present of a little piano. It's in the bungalow on the lot.

Now, I can't remember all the different things that happened at dancing school. I went there in 1932, almost four years ago. I was just three years old then, so all of those things happened in the middle of my life. And that's so long ago! So many other things have happened since that time, so many things that neither Mom, nor Daddy, nor my two brothers, nor the teacher at the dancing school, nor even I, ever ex-

MY LIFE AND TIMES

pected to happen, that—well, it's funny, Corky, but I sometimes think that it wasn't Shirley Temple at all who went to that school but some other little girl whom Mom or Daddy told me about.

But there's one day at school that I remember very well. It's the most important day in my life. Everybody says that if it hadn't turned out just the way it *did* turn out, then instead of acting at a big studio like I do now, and having my own bungalow, and knowing lots of stars, and getting so many letters and presents from children and grown-ups all over the world, why, I'd probably be just an ordinary little girl with pretty curls, getting ready to go to school for the first time.

MY LIFE AND TIMES

It was the beginning of the summer. My third birthday was on April 23, 1932; and my birthday party was past already. I was leaving the dancing class with Mom that day when we saw a whole crowd of mothers and their children waiting in one of the large halls of the dancing-school building. We could tell something unusual was going to take place because all the children were dressed up in their best clothes, and the mothers were all dressed up, too. Mom stopped and asked one of the women what was the matter. The woman seemed to be surprised that Mom hadn't heard. She said, "Why, Educational Pictures are sending around a director to pick out twenty-five children. They're going to make a series of

When we were on location at Sherwood Lake
I got my lunch from the studio truck.

MY LIFE AND TIMES

baby short subjects. All the children have to be between two and four, and they mustn't be taller than thirty-six inches—exactly one yard high. Shirley's just right, isn't she? Why don't you let her stay?"

The first thing that Mom said was no, she couldn't do that. I wasn't even dressed to see a director, she said. All I had on was my plain old dancing dress.

"That's a shame," said the other woman. "It's a chance to break into the studios. You might wait a long time before it happens again."

Mom started to walk away with me. I guess she couldn't make up her mind whether to go away or not because she stopped, then she went a little farther. I guess she kind of wanted to try to get me into the movies even though Daddy didn't like the idea. Finally she stopped. Then she said, "Oh, let's show them, even in your old clothes!"

So we went back again to where the crowd was waiting. I remember hearing one of the women saying to Mom, "Do you know, Mrs. Temple, that the man who's going to produce these pictures has advertised in the newspapers for child players? And he's already seen five thousand of them?"

Mom said, "And you're sure he isn't looking for children with screen experience? Shirley's never acted, you know. And she's just beginning to learn how to dance."

Just then the director and two or three

other men came in. Everybody became quiet right away. The teacher said, "This is Director Charles Lamont of Educational Pictures. I think he has a few words to say to all you ladies." Then Mr. Lamont stepped forward. He was a nice-looking man about Daddy's age with a little brown mustache. He said that he guessed everybody knew why he was there, and he wished all the mothers would please walk away for about ten minutes or so, because he wanted to speak to the children alone. Mom gave my curls a few twists with her fingers. She whispered to me, "If he asks you to dance, or asks you to sing, just do the way you always do, Presh."

People always ask me how I acted when

MY LIFE AND TIMES

I was with a director for the first time in my life. Did I feel nervous? Did I start crying? Did I run after my mother? They want to know if I went up to Mr. Lamont and smiled at him and said, "I'm Shirley Temple. You'd better let me show you how I can dance!" They keep saying, "Well, you must have done *something* to make him pick you out from among all the other children."

But I tell everybody that I didn't do anything at all except walk past Mr. Lamont. That's what all the children there did—just walked past him. I don't know why he picked me out. I didn't even know that he *had* picked me out until three or four days later when he telephoned Mom and told her to bring me to the studio for a screen test.

MY LIFE AND TIMES

And lots of people say, "I bet Mr. Lamont is your favorite director. Tell the truth, Shirley!" But that always makes me feel angry. I say, "I don't know who my favorite director is!" And that *is* the truth, Corky. When Mr. Lamont was my director, then *he* was my favorite director. And when Mr. Hamilton McFadden—I always call him Mr. "Ham" McFadden because that's what everybody else calls him—directed Warner Baxter, and Madge Evans, and John Boles, and Jimmy Dunn, and Stepin Fetchit, and me in *Stand Up and Cheer,* why, then *he* became my favorite director. Oh, I've got lots of favorite directors. There's Harry Lachman, and Alexander Hall—he made *Little Miss Marker* with Adolphe Menjou, Charles Bick-

I've been going to school since I was five.

Miss Barkley starts school every morning at nine.

MY LIFE AND TIMES

ford, and me—and Henry Hathaway, and Mr. John Robertson, who made *Our Little Girl,* and Irving Cummings, who made *Curly Top,* and jolly Mr. David Butler, who's my favorite director now because he just finished *The Littlest Rebel,* my latest picture.

Another thing that people are always asking me is, how did I feel while I was making my first screen test? I mostly always say, "I don't know how I felt." Or, "I guess I felt all right."

Come close to me, Corky. I'll whisper this in your ear. The day I made my first screen test I had the best time in my life. It was ever so much fun! I can't begin to tell you. I was never in a real film studio before. Neither was Mom. We were both excited. Mom was

MY LIFE AND TIMES

excited, because she didn't know what was going to happen when I made my test, or whether I would get scared and forget how to speak or something. And I was excited because the studio was so big and so wonderful. It was like a huge cave without any windows and with the ceiling high, high up—bigger than Aladdin's cave and the cave where the gnomes took little Snow White in the fairy book. I didn't know where to look first. There were other children in the studio that same day. They were also going to make screen tests, but none of us cared anything about tests. We just ran around the studio exploring. We pushed through doors, and scooted through make-believe houses, and jumped on chairs. We found hats that didn't

MY LIFE AND TIMES

fit us, and all kinds of ropes on the floor, and lamps that shone so brightly you got blind for a minute or two if you looked straight at them.

Then the funniest thing of all happened. Mr. Lamont, and a man named Mr. Hays (his first name was Jack, I think, and he was the producer) wanted us all to get undressed! You see, the pictures they were going to make were called *Baby Burlesks*. The whole cast—we were all little children—had to wear things that looked like diapers, with great big safety pins in front. So all the mothers undressed their children, and Mom undressed me, and we all ran around in our panties!

Then I made my screen test. This is what

I'd probably be just an ordinary little girl
with pretty curls.

MY LIFE AND TIMES

I had to do. I had to stand in front of the camera in my panties, and smile, and wink my eye, and shake my shoulder two or three times in a dance, and then say, *"Oui, mon cher!"* That's French, Corky. Can you imagine! The first words that I ever spoke before a camera were French! You see, the first of the *Baby Burlesks* was going to be a one-reel picture called *War Babies*. It was supposed to make fun of *What Price Glory*. The part that they were testing me for was Charmaine. Dolores Del Rio played that part in the big picture. I had to be a little French dancer in a cafe. So I had to speak my lines in French instead of in English. I'm studying French now with my teacher, Miss Barkley. I know that *"Oui, mon cher!"* means

MY LIFE AND TIMES

"Yes, my dear!" I didn't know what it meant then. Mr. Lamont told me to just go ahead and say it. So I just went ahead and said it, right into the "mike" over my head.

"I'll let you know in a few days what we've decided to do about Shirley," Mr. Lamont told Mom after the test was over.

If there are any little girls and boys reading this (or even any big girls and boys) I'd like them to know that making a screen test is easy as pie. It didn't scare me a bit. I felt fine. I wasn't nervous. Do you know who was nervous? Mom!

And do you know who was nervous after we got home? Daddy! I suppose you're pretty surprised to hear that. He didn't want me to get into the movies at all at first.

MY LIFE AND TIMES

But I guess he just didn't think that I had a chance, so he made up his mind it would be better not even to let us think about it. As soon as I made the screen test, though, he wanted me to get a part more than Mom did. He was so happy when Mr. Lamont finally called up and said that he was giving me the part of Charmaine in the first picture—and other parts in the next pictures if I made good in the first—that Daddy said that the movies were a wonderful thing and that he was going to go to every picture that his daughter ever made. And he has kept his promise. He's seen all my pictures, dozens of times!

Everybody calls me a screen veteran. Just a few days ago Janet Gaynor—the bungalow

MY LIFE AND TIMES

she uses in the studio is just across the street from mine, and she often drops in for a chat —told me that she counted up all the pictures I've made so far. The big ones, I mean. She found there were eight of them in about two years. "That's more than lots of grown-up stars make," she said. "You're a regular trouper, Shirley!"

So now I'll tell you something about acting. It isn't hard—not nearly so hard as reading, writing, or arithmetic. It's like playing a game of make-believe. That's the easiest game in the world to play. It is for me, anyway. You remember I told you I used to ride my tricycle down to the eucalyptus trees at the end of the garden and pretend that I had gone all the way to Chicago?

MY LIFE AND TIMES

Well, maybe I pretended, and maybe I really believed it. After a while it gets pretty hard to tell the difference. It's the same with acting for the movies. You pretend you're not Shirley Temple any more but the Little Colonel, or some other little girl. And you pretend so hard that pretty soon you don't know whether you're still pretending, or whether somehow or other you haven't become some other little girl.

Anybody can do that, I think. I know even when I'm not acting for a picture, I'm pretending just for the fun of it. From the little porch of my bungalow I can see a big steamship down at the end of the studio street. It isn't a real steamship. There's no water there. It's just a "prop" boat. They use it

You pretend you're not Shirley Temple any more, but some other little girl. In "Curly Top" I had to pretend I was a bride.

when they're making a picture. It looks just like a real ship when you see it on the screen. But it only has a front. It's flat. There's nothing in back. Well, I've often pretended I was on that ship, sailing far, far away. I went to lots of places. Oh, pretending is loads of fun!

Only you've got to pretend with all your might. Not very long ago, while I was rehearsing a scene for *The Little Colonel*, Mr. Butler, the director, held up his hand. "You're not putting enough life in that scene, Shirley!" he said. "Try it over again, please!" I didn't feel so good when Mr. Butler said that. I almost felt like crying. It kind of spoiled the game for a minute. But I tried it over again, as hard as I could. This

First you always ask who else is in the picture.
In "The Littlest Rebel" I played with
John Boles and Karen Morley.

MY LIFE AND TIMES

time Mr. Butler cried, "That's fine, darling! That's the way to do it!" I felt very happy all over again. But I knew that Mr. Butler was right about the first time. So after the scene was "shot" I went up to him and said in a very low voice, so that nobody else should hear me, "That first time *was* pretty faked, Mr. Butler. I thought so, too!" Then I smiled at him, as much as to say, *"We know, don't we?"*

And I think maybe he picked me up and kissed me. But I'm not sure.

I'm quite sure that I wouldn't know *what* to act if it weren't for Mom. She explains the story of every one of my pictures to me before I start working in them. I can remember she started to do that the day they

MY LIFE AND TIMES

decided to let me have my first part in *War Babies*. Mr. Lamont or somebody gave her a script of the picture. We went and sat in a corner of the studio, where it was quiet. She read it over herself. It took her only a few minutes. The whole picture was only one reel. That means it would take just about ten or eleven minutes to run on the screen. You can see how short that was when you think that the pictures I'm in now take more than an hour to run. Well, after she read the script, she told me the story. She kept saying, "Do you understand, Presh? Do you understand?"

I guess lots of mothers tell their children the stories they read in books, when their children don't know how to read yet. And

Joel McCrea is fine for piggy-back rides.

MY LIFE AND TIMES

I guess almost all children act out the stories by themselves later when they're alone, or with their playmates. The only difference is that instead of acting them out like that, I do it in front of a camera with lots of grown-ups around!

And—oh yes, there's one other thing! You've got to remember just what to say. That's one of the most important parts of the game. But that's not hard, either. Here, just let me tell you what to do. It's what I do now, and it works fine.

First you go home with your mother from the studio. While she's driving along you get her to tell you the story of the new picture you're going to do. But before she even starts to do that, you ask her to tell you who

MY LIFE AND TIMES

else is going to be in the picture. Because you always like to know beforehand whether you're going to see a lot of Jimmy Dunn (you can always do a dance with him between "shots"), or Joel McCrea (he's fine for piggy-back rides), or Mr. Lionel Barrymore (he's always dozing off in his chair while waiting to go on the set, and you can say boo! and wake him up again), or Claire Trevor, or Rochelle Hudson, or Rosemary Ames (you can always depend on *them* for ice cream with chocolate gravy), or anybody else.

Then you find out whether Mr. Butler is going to direct, or Mr. Cummings, or somebody else you don't know yet. When that's all settled, you're ready to hear the story.

MY LIFE AND TIMES

Sometimes you ask questions in the middle of it, such as "What's a colonel?" Or, "Why does Mr. McCrea keep on loving his wife when she treats him like that?" You have to know those things. Once when we were getting ready to work on *Stand Up and Cheer,* I asked Mom: "What's a politician?" and she had quite a job explaining it to me, Corky.

Well, after you get home, and you eat your dinner, and your Daddy gives you a bath, and you get into your pajamas, and sit in the bathroom while your Mom fixes your curls for the night—why, when all that's finished, you finally slide into your bed and pull the covers up and you say, "Okay, Mom! I'm ready." Then Mom closes the door and sits

I asked Mom, "What's a politician?"

MY LIFE AND TIMES

on the edge of the bed with the script book in her hand. She reads the lines you've got to know for the "call" the next morning. Sometimes there is a whole page of them, and sometimes even more! They're all part of the story that Mom told you about already. So you know what they all mean, pretty much. You repeat them after Mom, word for word, five or six times. She might say: "You're supposed to feel very happy when you say this line, Presh." So you smile and try to feel happy when you say it. Or, "You're supposed to be eating a thick sandwich while you're saying these lines." So you try to sound as if you're chewing and swallowing pieces of sandwich while you're speaking. Then Mom closes the script book,

MY LIFE AND TIMES

and you know that's all you have to remember for the next day's call.

You say your prayers and Mom puts out the lights. Then maybe you say some of the lines over again to yourself in the dark room, just for good measure. And when you wake up the next morning, you know them all!

When I start going to school, Corky, and I have to memorize recitations to say in the assembly, I'm going to use the same scheme. Only I'll be able to read by myself then. I'll need Mom, though, to check me on the lines, and to tell me about the action. You ought to know that Mom's a pretty fine director herself. I guess she does as much work in directing me in the pictures I'm making now as the directors who get the credit for it. She

MY LIFE AND TIMES

hardly ever interferes when we are on the set. It is when we're in the bungalow, or at home, that she starts working. The Fox Company pays her a big salary, too, for being my own private director. I heard Daddy once tell some friends of ours at home that with his salary at the bank and Mom's salary at the studio they were able to buy our new house, and keep Jack and Sonny in school, and take care of me. Daddy says he's saving all the money I make in his bank for me when I grow up.

Mr. Will Rogers used to call Mom my manager. One day, while she and I were eating lunch together in the studio cafe, Mr. Rogers stopped over at our table. He pointed at my plate of vegetables, and shook his

MY LIFE AND TIMES

head, and said, "So *you* have to eat that old rabbit food while your Manager eats steak. That's a great set-up!" I told Mr. Rogers that it wasn't rabbit food, and I liked it even if it was—all except the onions.

Now, let's see, Corky, where was I in my story? Oh, yes, I was up to the part about beginning to make the short-subjects for Educational Pictures. The first one, the one that made fun of *What Price Glory,* was started in the beginning of the summer of 1932. I was just a little over three years old then, and that's more than three years ago. Mom went with me to the studio, of course. She wasn't as excited as she was when we went for the screen test, but she was much happier. I guess she always thought it

Mr. Will Rogers was a very good friend of mine.

would be fun for me to get into the movies, even though she pretended all the while that she didn't care whether I did or not. Maybe she wanted to get into the movies herself when she was a little girl.

I didn't have many lines to say in that first picture—just a dozen or so—and half of them were in French. I had to do a dance. I shook my shoulders to the music and made roly-poly eyes. I wore those diaper-things with the big safety pin in front that I told you about; and a silk waist like the one that Dolores Del Rio wore in *What Price Glory*. It kept slipping off one shoulder all the time.

But do you know what happened in that picture? I kissed a boy for the first time in my life! No, I kissed two of them!

I wore those diaper-things with the big safety pin in front, and a silk waist. It kept slipping off one shoulder all the time.

MY LIFE AND TIMES

So you can't say that I didn't have any sweethearts. One boy's name was Jean Butler and the other boy's name was Georgie Smith. They were about four years old. They were very handsome boys, even in their diapers! They wanted to marry me, both of them! So I kissed them and said I would. I don't know what's become of them now. I don't see them any more.

Oh, I've been in love lots of times since then. I fell in love with Jimmy Dunn the minute I saw him. He was in the cast of the first big picture I played in, *Stand Up and Cheer*. He fell in love with me right away, too. He told me lots of times that he loved me better than any other girl in the world. I believed him. Wouldn't you?

MY LIFE AND TIMES

And one day he picked me up and kissed me, right in front of Mom!

Then there's Mr. Lionel Barrymore—I was in love with him, too. He's not really as old as he looked in *The Little Colonel*. He was wearing a white wig in that picture. I was afraid to tell him that I liked him. I thought maybe he would frown at me. I asked Mom what to do. She told me he would probably be very pleased to know that I liked him, and to tell him the very first chance I got.

But do you know what I had to do? I had to throw mud at his beautiful white palm beach suit. It was in the script that way. Oh, how I hated to do it! How can you throw mud at anybody you like! And especially when he's wearing a palm beach suit! And worse than anything, when he's wearing a wig as white as snow! I couldn't do it at all, Corky. I picked up a handful of gooey mud and raised my hand, but I couldn't throw it. Mr. Butler shouted, "Throw it, Shirley! What are you waiting for?" I was ashamed to tell him that I loved Mr. Barrymore too much to throw mud at him. But what do you suppose! Mr. Barrymore said, all at once, "All right, Shirley, let's have that mud, the whole handful, and throw it hard—get it *all* over the suit!"

What could I do, Corky? I had to throw it. It got all over his white suit and some of it got in his white hair. As soon as the scene was finished I ran up to him. "Oh,

Mr. Lionel Barrymore is not really as old as he looked in "The Little Colonel." He was wearing a white wig in that picture.

MY LIFE AND TIMES

I'm so sorry, Mr. Barrymore, that I had to throw that mud at you!" He just smiled, and made a deep bow and kissed my hand. Then he said very slowly, "There must be ten million men in this country who would let you throw mud at their best Sunday suits and consider it an honor. I'm one of them, little lady!" Now wasn't that lovely?

I fell in love with Gary Cooper, too. Only he was much too tall for me, so I gave him up.

My latest sweethearts are Joel McCrea and Poodles Hanneford. I can't make up my mind which one I'll marry. I met both of them while we were making *Our Little Girl*. Poodles Hanneford isn't a poodle, Corky; he's a clown—an English clown. When he

MY LIFE AND TIMES

does tricks on a horse you laugh so hard that your sides hurt. He's much funnier than an elephant eating peanuts. He knows lots of other clowns, too. If I married him, it would be like going to the circus all the time. You can have lots of fun with Joel McCrea, though. He's got the nicest shoulders to ride piggy-back on of anybody in Hollywood. One day while we were out on location at Sherwood Lake—that's not far from Los Angeles—making the picnic scenes for *Our Little Girl,* he gave me a piggy-back ride. As I sat way up there, I wrapped the edges of my dress around the front of his head, so that he looked as if he were wearing an old grandma's cap. And when Rosemary Ames, and Lyle Talbot, and Miss

MY LIFE AND TIMES

Erin O'Brien-Moore, and Mr. Robertson, the director, and the script girl, and the cameraman, and Mom, and all the people in the company saw us, they shouted with laughter. "Look at old Mother McCrea!" they laughed. "Look at Shirley riding on old Mother McCrea!"

And I laughed as hard as any of them, and so did Joel McCrea.

And those are my sweethearts—except for Daddy, who's been my best sweetheart ever since I can remember. He's very happy now. But he wasn't always happy. While I was making the first little short-subject a long while ago—I've often heard Mom say to people that I didn't get paid more than about forty or fifty dollars a picture—Dad

Daddy's been my best sweetheart ever since I can remember. What a fine time we had on the ship!

MY LIFE AND TIMES

got bad news from the bank. He never told me what it was, but I heard him talking to Mom. I could see by his face that it was something very, very bad. And then one day he stayed home from the bank. It was the first time I ever saw him do that except on Sundays. I asked him why, and he said President Roosevelt had closed all the banks, and he couldn't go to work.

We sat out in the garden of our old house in Santa Monica. I can't remember what day of the week it was exactly, except that it wasn't a Sunday.

I don't know the reason why, Corky, but the garden was always different in the middle of the week. It was quieter than on Sunday. Daddy and I sat down on the

MY LIFE AND TIMES

bench near the little wooden playhouse that I used to have. He looked kind of upset. He didn't know just what to do. So I decided to cheer him up.

I wanted to climb into his lap and say, "I love you very much, Daddy." But just then Mom came out of the house and said we had to leave right away for the studio. So we all got into Daddy's old car—it was the only car we could get into because he didn't have a new one!—and he drove us to the studio. I sat between him and Mom on the front seat. Nobody talked much. Only when we came to the front of the studio and Mom and I got off, he looked at me with a funny little smile and said it was a mighty good thing *somebody* in the Temple family

MY LIFE AND TIMES

was working, even if *he* wasn't! Oh, if he had only known the good luck we were going to have by that Christmas! How happy he'd have been!

I got my first part in a big picture then, Corky. And a few months later I became a moving picture working-lady like Janet Gaynor, and Greta Garbo, and Jean Harlow!

I'll tell you how it all came about. Lots of people keep asking me to tell them this story all the time. They say, "Nobody ever heard of Shirley Temple two years ago. Where did you come from all of a sudden?" It wasn't so "all of a sudden" as it sounds. And it wasn't so easy, either. I almost didn't become anything at all.

You see, one day not long after the time

Then I became a moving picture working-lady.
Here is how I "worked" in "Now and Forever."

MY LIFE AND TIMES

Daddy stayed home because the banks were closed, Mom found out that we weren't going to make any more of those one-reel *Baby Burlesks* I was telling you about. The director told her that there were seven of them made already. He said that the public didn't seem to care very much for them—not nearly as much as they cared for the *Our Gang Comedies*. Besides, all the children in the cast of the *Baby Burlesks* were growing up. We were supposed to be only thirty-six inches high; but I was nearly forty inches myself, and some of the boys were even taller than that! We were getting entirely too big to be able to wear those diaper-things we all had to wear in the pictures. So that was the end of the series. I said good-bye to

I was nearly forty inches high myself.

the other children. We were all good friends by that time. We had been working together in the little pictures for more than a year. They were almost the only playmates I had.

One little girl I liked best of all. She's the only child that I still see a great deal of. She's always around when I'm making a picture. She was on the set while I was making *Baby Take a Bow*, and *Stand Up and Cheer*, and *Little Miss Marker*, and *Now and Forever*, and *Bright Eyes*, and *The Little Colonel*, and *Our Little Girl*, and *Curly Top*, and *The Littlest Rebel*. And I guess she'll be around on the sets of the pictures I make after those. Do you know why, Corky? Because I have to have a stand-in.

I'll explain to you what a stand-in is.

MY LIFE AND TIMES

She's a little girl who's just your size, and who can wear the same clothes that you do in your pictures. She's something like your twin sister, only she doesn't have to look *exactly* like you—I mean, her face can be different. Well, that's what a stand-in is. Now I'll tell you what a stand-in does. I know all about it, Corky, because I've seen it myself many times—and anyhow Jimmy Dunn, who's a very good friend of mine, told me about it, too. When you're all through "shooting" a scene, then the cameraman, and the sound-man, and the electricians start fixing up the new scene. That often takes quite a long time. And the cameraman wants the star to sit in the exact place where she's going to sit for her next scene,

One little girl I liked best of all. She's my stand-in. That's something like a twin sister, only she doesn't have to look exactly like you.

MY LIFE AND TIMES

o that he can aim his camera just right.
And the sound-man wants her to sit there,
too, so he can fix the mike at just the right
spot. And the electricians want her there,
so they can make the lights shine just right.

But the star is generally too busy to sit
there. She has to have her curls combed, or
her dress straightened out, or a new one put
on, or she has to drink a glass of milk, or run
a race with Stepin Fetchit—he can run like
lightning when he wants to!—or practice
a new dance routine with Jack Donohue, or
hum over a new song with Mom. So your
stand-in does it in your place. It's not such
a nice job, I think. Because lots of times you
have to sit very still with the hot lights shining right in your eyes.

MY LIFE AND TIMES

But, do you know, Corky, that every day Mom gets letters from other mothers all over the country, and from Europe, too, with pictures of their little girls? The mothers write and say, "Doesn't my little girl look just like Shirley? She'd love to be Shirley's stand-in. Won't you please let her?" But Mom can't, because I already have a stand-in.

Soon Daddy went back to the bank again. One day I heard him saying to Mom that things seemed to be getting worse instead of better, and that she needn't be surprised if he got another cut. They didn't think I understood what he was saying. They always stopped talking when Jack or Sonny was around.

Mom tried to get me parts at some of the

MY LIFE AND TIMES

other studios. But nobody needed me much. I worked one or two days in different little pictures.

Daddy said there was no use bothering about the movies any longer. He said that I had about three hundred dollars in the bank—that was all the money I made working for a whole year in the seven little pictures—and he thought that would be enough when I grew up to keep me in college for one term anyway. Mom, though, was sorry I couldn't get anything to do at the studios. She kept saying she wished I could get a contract or something—she didn't care about the money—just so long as I had a chance to get a good part when it came along some day.

MY LIFE AND TIMES

Now Mom says that all those studios that could have signed me up for about fifty dollars a week are good and sorry that they didn't when they had the chance.

About the end of the summer Mom got a telephone call from Educational Pictures. They said they were going to start a new series of short subjects called *Frolics of Youth*. They had a part for me in them. Mom took it right away. I didn't get a contract, though. I was just supposed to make one picture, and then—if everything went okay—they would ask me to make another one. The players were almost all high-school boys and girls, and there were some grown-ups. I was cast as the little sister of one of the boys. I was the youngest one in

This is my bungalow at the studio, with small rooms and small furniture for me. I rest and study here.

MY LIFE AND TIMES

the company. I was four and a half years old then.

This is a very funny thing, Corky, and you ought to know about it. I've made quite a few pictures. But I don't get taken to the movies often. Daddy and Mom hardly ever used to go to the movies at all, I guess, until I got into them; I know Daddy didn't, because he told me so. I think the first movie I saw in my life was Mickey Mouse. I still like him best of all. I met Mr. Walt Disney at the Academy banquet last year. I told him how much I liked Mickey. "Very well," said Mr. Disney, "I'll send him around to you. If you like him as much as you say you do, you can keep him." The next day Mickey came. He wasn't flat the way he is

MY LIFE AND TIMES

on the screen. He was stuffed, like a teddy bear. I've got his sweetheart, Minnie, too. They both sit next to Joe Penner's duck in my doll cabinet.

Mom says that the first time I saw myself on the screen in a little theater in our neighborhood, I laughed and clapped my hands. She kept whispering to me, "Do you see yourself? That's you, Presh! That's *you!*" A person looks awfully funny on the screen. And you get the queerest feeling, Corky, when you hear yourself speak. Your voice sounds so terribly loud that you feel like saying, "Sh-h-h, Shirley—you'll wake everybody up!"

Daddy was with us that first night. He was so happy after the picture was over that he looked as if he were crying. I see all of my new pictures right on the lot, now, in a tiny little movie theater. That's like a regular movie theater except that you don't pay anything to get in, and there aren't any ushers, and you can shout to the man in the booth, "All right—let's see it!" That means he can put out the lights and start the picture.

This is how I got my *big* chance, Corky. Mom heard one day that Mr. George White was looking for some little girls for one of the singing and dancing numbers in the *Scandals,* which he was going to make for Fox Pictures. There was a "call" at his office on the lot, and we went. We found about three hundred other little girls there with

I thought it would be fun to make my lamb go to school, too, but he didn't want to come.

MY LIFE AND TIMES

their mothers, and many of them with their agents—so we couldn't get very near Mr. White. Mom was quite disappointed. But a man finally came over to us. He said he was an assistant director and his name was Leo Houck. He told Mom he recognized me from seeing me in the *Baby Burlesks*. He thought I was grand. He said something ought to be done about me. He told Mom he didn't think there was much use in expecting me to get a part in Mr. White's *Scandals*. The "call" was only to see what little girls they could get if they really made up their minds that they wanted any. Nothing was decided *yet*. But Mr. Houck said other pictures would be coming along soon where he was pretty sure they might need a little girl

Brother Jack told me that a bicycle has two wheels.
And the Los Angeles policemen decided I should have
License Number One.

MY LIFE AND TIMES

like me. In the meantime he wanted to see the *Frolics of Youth.*

Then one night after Daddy and Mom and I saw a preview of the second one of the *Frolics of Youth* at a theater in Beverly Hills, Mr. Houck came up to us in the lobby. He had another man with him named Jay Gorney, who was a song writer. Mr. Gorney told Daddy and Mom that Mr. Will Rogers and somebody else had just thought up an idea for a big musical story, and Mr. Sheehan was going to produce it with lots of important people in the cast. He said Warner Baxter, Madge Evans, John Boles, Jimmy Dunn, Ralph Morgan, Nigel Bruce, and Stepin Fetchit were in the cast already.

There would also be a spot in the picture,

MY LIFE AND TIMES

he said, for a little girl to play the part of Jimmy Dunn's daughter. It wasn't much of a part, he told us—just a few cute lines—but maybe a smart little girl could do something with them. He said if Mom brought me to the studio the next day he would introduce me to Lew Brown, who was going to write the music and some of the lyrics and dialogue for the story, and would also help Mr. Sheehan produce it. It would be a very good idea for me to meet Mr. Brown anyway, he said, because he was the man who "discovered" Jackie Cooper—I knew who Jackie was from seeing the picture *Skippy*—and perhaps now Mr. Brown could "discover" me.

We all laughed at that, especially Daddy,

MY LIFE AND TIMES

who said wasn't it a shame Columbus was dead, because then *he* could "discover" me too!

Well, we met Mr. Lew Brown at the studio. Mom sat and smiled while Mr. Houck and Mr. Gorney told him about my other pictures. Then Mr. Brown said, "Let's see what you can do, Shirley." So somebody played the "St. Louis Blues" on a piano and I did a buck-and-wing for him. Then I sang a song that I had heard Rudy Vallee croon over the radio a few days before. He was surprised, all right. That settled it, Mr. Brown said. He would sign me for the part right away. So he really *did* "discover" me after all, you see!

We certainly thanked Mr. Houck, though!

I fell in love with Gary Cooper, too.

MY LIFE AND TIMES

He said Hollywood wasn't finished with me just yet. A good deal more would happen before the picture was finished. He was sure of that.

Oh, it was fun working at a big studio like Fox, Corky. Daddy drove us there early in the morning on his way to work. There were policemen at the gates. They all know me now. But at that time they'd stop us and say, "Who are you? Where do you want to go?" Then Daddy or Mom would say, "This is our little girl, Shirley Temple. She's working in Stage 8 this morning in *Stand Up and Cheer*. Here is her pass." Then they'd let us through.

At one part of the studio you went under a narrow bridge. When you came out on

MY LIFE AND TIMES

the other side you were in a funny old village. The houses weren't like ordinary houses. They were made of brown stone with high slanty roofs like dunce-caps, and little windows way, way up, and queer old chimneys with no smoke in them. Mom said they were French and German and Italian houses—not real ones, just "props." Nobody ever lived in them. But people really did stay in the pretty little houses in the American part of the studio. "Look, Presh!" Mom said to me one morning. "There's Lilian Harvey's bungalow. Isn't it beautiful!" It was beautiful, all right. It was all blue and rose, with very green grass on both sides, and a fence all around it. Instead of a number, it had a name in French. It was

Mr. Sheehan gave me a little piano.
It's in the bungalow on the lot.

MY LIFE AND TIMES

called *La Maison de Reves*. My teacher, Miss Barkley, says that means "Dream House." I guess that was a good name for it.

Mom keeps saying it's *my* Dream House come true. Do you know why? Because it belongs to me now!

Jimmy Dunn was the first big star I ever worked with. I had to learn a song and dance routine to do with him for *Stand Up and Cheer*. There's nothing to be afraid of when you work with big stars. They're just like other people. We rehearsed the dance in the gymnasium. Sometimes we went off into one of the empty stages because all the girls in the chorus would begin rehearsing their steps in the gymnasium and there wasn't much room for us.

MY LIFE AND TIMES

Mom always went with us. She just sat on the side and watched. When I looked over at her she smiled. If I did a wrong step, she shook her head a little. The only time she scolded was when I wouldn't want to stop to take a rest. But then Jimmy Dunn made me stop. Mom still sits on the side and watches me when I rehearse for my new pictures and when I shoot them, too. I don't ever want her to go away. I feel too all alone then, and I begin to cry.

There were so many important stars in *Stand Up and Cheer*—I mean Warner Baxter and John Boles and Madge Evans and Nigel Bruce and Aunt Jemima and Jimmy Dunn and Ralph Morgan—and so many beautiful dancing girls, and so many other

MY LIFE AND TIMES

little girls and boys about my age who also had bits in the picture, that nobody paid very much attention to me. It wasn't anything like the attention they pay to me now. But what a difference there was after Mr. Sheehan saw me on the screen in the little movie theater on the lot!

They told us later that he shouted, "She's stolen the picture!" That doesn't mean anything bad, Corky. It's just a way of saying that nobody expected my little bit to be very important and it turned out to be the best part in the whole picture.

Mr. Sheehan wanted to see us right away in his private office. Mom took me there. He shook my hand. He sat me on top of his desk. He called me Shirley. He had kind of gray hair, but his cheeks were red and he didn't look old at all. He said, "In a little while, darling, you're going to make millions of people happy—sick people, sad people, poor people—yes, and rich people and young people, too. You'll make everyone who sees you happy. They'll all love you. You're going to be the most loved little girl in the whole world!"

We took a taxi all the way home that night. It was the first time we did it. It cost a lot of money. But Mom said we could celebrate now!

I'll tell you something, Corky. I've heard Mom and Daddy say that even after I signed my contract—you know I signed it with a big X instead of my name because I couldn't

I signed my contract with a big X instead of my name because I couldn't write yet.

MY LIFE AND TIMES

write yet!—nobody really thought that so many people would like me as much as they do today.

One day, not long after my first picture was finished, a boy came to Mom at the studio and said there were some letters for me in the mail room. So we hurried over to the mail room and they gave us a little package of letters. We went and sat down somewhere and Mom opened them. They were all from people we didn't know who saw me on the screen. They wrote to tell me how much they liked me. Some of them asked me to send them photographs with my own name signed to them.

Mom felt very happy and proud to get the letters. They meant that people were

This is my play corner. And Grumpy is my best bear!

MY LIFE AND TIMES

beginning to notice me. Big stars like Janet Gaynor, Mary Pickford, Charlie Chaplin, and even Mickey Mouse get hundreds of letters every week. Do you know how many letters I get now, Corky? About a thousand a day!

At first, when there weren't so many, Mom and Daddy thought they would take care of them after dinner. But soon they couldn't. Miss Dorothy Drum, my secretary, answers them now. But Mom and Daddy still read lots of them—especially those that come from far-off places like India and Japan and China. On holidays like Christmas, Easter, St. Valentine's Day, and April 23 (that's my birthday!), I get more letters than on regular days. Packages

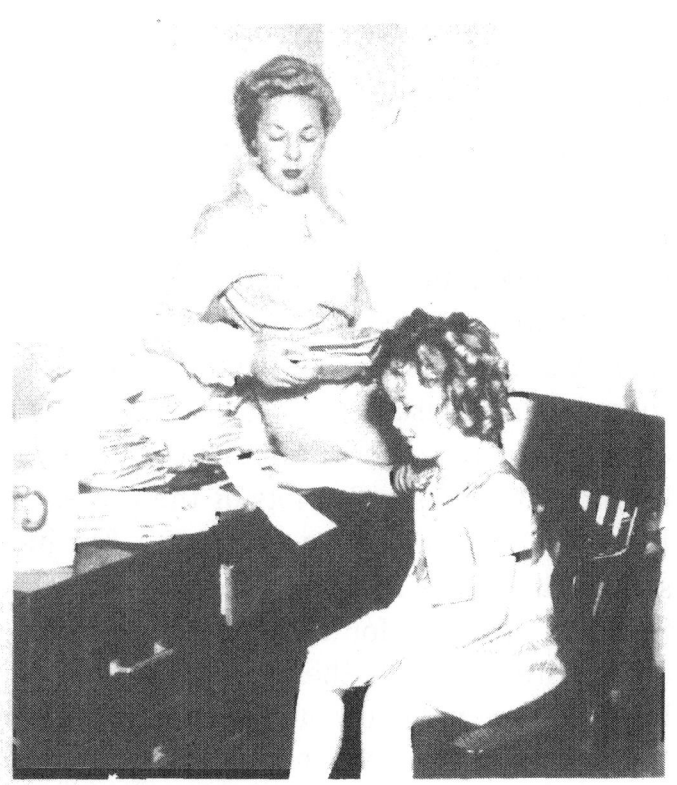

I get about a thousand letters a day now!

MY LIFE AND TIMES

with presents come, too! I always like to open the packages myself and be surprised. Dolls are in most of them, or doll clothes. But I also get dozens of different kinds of picture books and games.

If we kept all the presents that I keep getting, Corky, there soon wouldn't be any room in this house for us. So we give most of them away to the hospitals and to the Community Chest. But lots of the presents I wouldn't give away for anything. For instance, there are the five rabbits that Mr. Sheehan gave me for Easter. We've built a big wire hutch for them in the garden in back of the bungalow at the studio. The twin turtles who live in the glass bowl—they're from Jimmy Dunn—can't be given

MY LIFE AND TIMES

away either because they've got my name painted on their backs. And there's Rowdy, the cocker spaniel. He's a Christmas present.

Why, Corky, you're a present yourself, you know! A friend of Mom's gave you to me when you were just a little puppy. How would you feel if I gave *you* away! And do you know why I call you Corky? Because your head is shaped just like a little round cork!

Oh, my dolls are *so* beautiful—like ladies all dressed for a party! How many have I got? I have twenty-eight. And those are only the ones we didn't give away. When we moved into our new house, Mom gave me a room just for my dolls. She told the

I had to have a place where I could take a nap, so my bungalow has this little-girl couch in it.

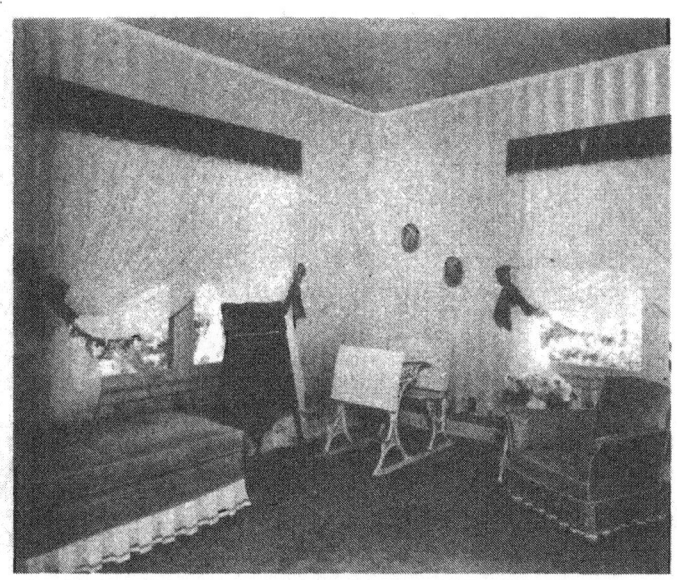

This is a corner of the living room of my bungalow on the lot and I spend most of my spare time here.

MY LIFE AND TIMES

carpenter to build a cupboard with glass doors all along one side of the room. Today some of the dolls sit on the shelves with their dresses spread out over their knees, and some of them stand. They all seem to be looking out of the windows of their own little house at me. I don't take them out very often, only when I have a party. Of course, whenever grown-up company come to the house, I take them up to see my dolls right away. But even then we don't take them out unless somebody really wants to see them very close.

I have "Shirley Temple" dolls that look like me and are dressed like me—or I'm dressed like *them,* I don't know which—and a rubber baby-doll that cries out loud

MY LIFE AND TIMES

and a couple of painted dolls that do tricks on a bar much better than Jack and Sonny could do on *their* bar in the garden of the old house.

Of all the people I know, Mr. Sheehan has given me the most presents. His biggest and best present is the studio bungalow. I'll tell you how he came to give it to me. When you're five years old you get good and sleepy in the afternoon. And even though you're supposed to act in a picture, you can't keep your eyes from closing. You have to take a nap. Well, you can take a fine nap right on your Mom's lap in one of the sound stages, or on a couch in your dressing room, or even in a big chair on one of the sets. But generally somebody who doesn't know

MY LIFE AND TIMES

you're taking a nap starts talking, or a carpenter begins to hammer nails, or music starts playing. That wakes you up.

Well, Mr. Sheehan heard about that. And he also heard about what used to happen every day when Mom took me over to the studio lunch room to eat. It's really a beautiful lunch room, Corky, with pictures painted on the walls and the nicest dinnertime smell. All the writers and directors and actors and actresses and "extras" and cameramen, and people who work in the different departments in the studio, eat there. When I'd walk in with Mom, they'd all look up and smile at me. They'd keep looking and smiling even after we sat down. And while I was eating, some of them would

MY LIFE AND TIMES

come over to say hello to me. Lots of them would bring other actors and actresses over to meet me. They'd stand around watching me eat. They'd laugh and joke. I'd laugh, too. Oh, it was plenty of fun. Only Mom said it wasn't the way a little girl ought to eat.

So Mr. Sheehan said I had to have a place where I could take a nap and eat my lunch away from my "public," and he gave me the bungalow that Lilian Harvey used to have before she left for Europe. First he had it all changed, though. He took out all the big furniture and put in little furniture. The new wall paper has pictures of Mickey Mouse and Humpty-Dumpty and lots of Mother Goose people all over it, which

MY LIFE AND TIMES

Lilian Harvey's wall paper never had. Even the bathroom is made especially small for me. Then he gave me a little piano to practice my songs on. I can take a nap now on my own couch in the living room, and eat my lunch on the white enamel table in the kitchen. Mom still makes my lunch, just as she always did. I can call anybody I like on my own telephone (and I do!) and pick flowers in my own garden just outside the window.

Just after I finished making *Bright Eyes*, I began going to school. Do you know where my schoolhouse is? Right inside the bungalow. I have a regular school desk painted white. It stands under the window in a separate room. That's my classroom.

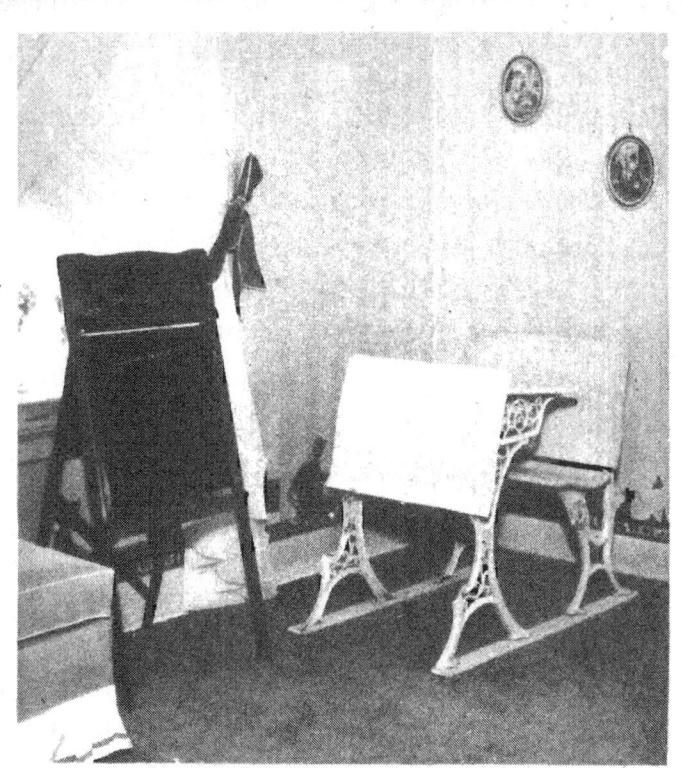

My school desk is painted white.
It stands under the window.

MY LIFE AND TIMES

But don't think I can come to school any time I please and stop whenever I feel like it. Oh, no. Miss Barkley starts school at nine o'clock. She doesn't bother calling the roll, because all she has to do is look over at me and she can see that I'm present. Then she closes the door of the classroom, and nobody can come in until I'm all through with my lessons at twelve o'clock. I've been going to school since I was a little over five. Not long ago a lady from the Los Angeles Board of Education examined me. She said that I knew enough to be in the third or fourth grade of public school.

Daddy is still manager of the bank in Los Angeles. And things aren't getting worse —they're getting better! He tells every-

I get dozens of picture books, and now I can read them to Mom, instead of Mom reading them to me.

MY LIFE AND TIMES

body that more people come to his bank now than ever did before. Their first reason for coming is to find out what Shirley Temple's father looks like. Then they decide that he looks all right, so what do they do but start saving their money at his bank! Why, Daddy has just got a big raise. He's very happy.

Jack's trying to make up his mind now whether to be a doctor or an engineer. *I* think he ought to be a doctor. Then he can go around holding people's hands and looking at his watch. Right now, Corky, he's going to Stanford University.

Sonny doesn't know yet just exactly what he wants to be. He's sixteen. He wears a cadet's uniform at his school in New Mexico.

MY LIFE AND TIMES

He comes home for all the holidays. Last summer when he came home he said he had decided to be a rancher and ride a horse all day. But the time before that he was all set to be a banker like Daddy. So you can't tell *what* he'll be.

Neither Sonny nor Jack wants to be a movie star. They can't even sing or dance, and have never acted in a single picture. They could have had parts in *David Copperfield,* maybe, because the director sent around for them to come to the studio for a try-out. But they ran out of the house before anyone could even talk to them. They're both pretty proud of me. But you'd never be able to tell that I was anything but their little sister, when we're all

Jack and Sonny are both pretty proud of me but you'd never be able to tell I was anything but their little sister.

MY LIFE AND TIMES

eating dinner home by ourselves. Jack still takes the biggest piece of pie; and if I didn't act quick, I guess he or Sonny would snitch my piece, too. Jack calls me Sis.

Mom is the busiest one of all of us now; even busier than I am, I guess. She's with me all the time—on the set when I'm acting, in the gym when I'm learning a new dance routine, in the bungalow, and home again at night. She dresses me. She even helps make most of the new dresses I wear in my pictures. She cooks my lunch at the studio. She plays the piano while I learn my songs. She teaches me all my lines, and explains just what the director wants me to do on the set. She drives our car. She talks to all the people who want to see me. She watches over me. I guess she gets worried sometimes, Corky, that I might get hurt when I go sailing on my swing, or riding piggyback downstairs from my doll room, or turning somersaults on the mat in the gym. One day last summer I begged to go riding on a pony with another little girl. A cowboy rode along with us. But all at once the little girl slipped off. She didn't get hurt. Oh, you can't imagine how frightened poor Mom was. She kept saying, "Suppose your horse had thrown you, too! Suppose you both had got hurt!"

Almost everyone who speaks to Mom always wants to know: Am I being spoiled by being in Hollywood? Can I really play and have fun and be "natural" like any

I guess Mom gets worried sometimes that I might get hurt when I go swinging.

MY LIFE AND TIMES

other little girl my age? What kind of a girl am I going to be when I grow up?

I'll tell you what I really think about myself, Corky. I think I'm having a fine time. I mean—*most* of the time. Oh, no, I don't *always* have fun. Mom and Daddy and most of the other folks who know me say, "Oh, Shirley thinks acting for the movies is like playing a game!" Well, I don't think it's *exactly* like playing a game. It's more like going to school—like learning how to read and write. It's something you're *supposed* to do. I can tell that everybody—the director, Mom, and all the actors and actresses—want me to sing, or dance, or speak my lines *just right,* not any old way. They're disappointed when I don't. I can tell it on

And here's Rowdy—he's a Christmas present.

MY LIFE AND TIMES

their faces, even though they don't ever scold me or anything. I feel disappointed, too. But when I do things right—why, then they're all as glad as can be. And I'm so happy I could hug and kiss them all!

It isn't easy to learn my "movie lessons." Before I played in *Curly Top* I had to know how to do a "rope tap routine." That means doing a tap dance while you're jumping rope. Well, I guess most little girls learn to jump rope while they're playing with their friends on the sidewalks. It's really a game for them. It wasn't for me. I had to go to the gym and Jack Donohue, who teaches me dancing, gave me a rope and showed me how to jump, right from the beginning. Imagine having a big man teach a

I went into the rabbit-hutch back of my bungalow
and said good-bye to all my rabbits.

MY LIFE AND TIMES

little girl how to jump rope! That's funny, isn't it?

But now I *can* jump rope, and it *is* fun, even though it was hard work at first and my legs felt like little pokers the day after the first lesson. And I can do a tap step, too, while I'm jumping. Wouldn't lots of little girls like to know how to do that? But the best part of all is this: Now I take my rope with me all over. I jump rope in the bungalow, and in the patio at home, and on the set with my stand-in. It's a game for me now, all right.

People don't pet me very much. You see, they don't get much chance to come around me now that I have my own bungalow to go to after I leave the set. Mr. Sheehan doesn't

MY LIFE AND TIMES

want too many people around. He doesn't even want me to go on "personal appearances" in different cities. He says crowds aren't good for little girls. I don't mind. Neither do Mom and Daddy. We enjoy being by ourselves.

One of the best times I ever had was when I made mud pies with Avonne Jackson and Nyanza Potts—they're both little colored children—while we were screening *The Little Colonel*. We didn't make them for the camera, either! Oh, no—they were just for us! And another time I had fun was when we made *Bright Eyes*. Jane Withers was in that picture with me. She's about ten or eleven. She was supposed to act very mean to me during the picture. But the

I think I'm having a fine time—most of the time!

MY LIFE AND TIMES

minute we had a rest period between scenes, she came running over to me and threw her arms around my neck and cried, "Oh, Shirley, I'm *so* sorry I had to act so bad to you!" I said that was all right. Then we both hurried out into the garden where they kept the beautiful doll-carriage that Jane wheeled around in the picture. The "prop-men" didn't want to give it to us at first, but after we begged them for a while they finally did let us have it. Then Jane said that I could wheel it all by myself, wherever I liked. Then I wheeled it round and round, and Jane walked beside me with one hand on it. Oh, we were such good friends! It was lovely fun.

But the best time I ever had in all my life

MY LIFE AND TIMES

was last summer when Mom and Daddy and I went to Honolulu. It was wonderful, Corky. You can't imagine how far out in the ocean we had to sail before we found Honolulu. My goodness, I thought we'd never get there.

Daddy had the idea first. I can't remember when he started talking about it. But I guess it was months and months before we went. He said we could go there on my vacation. "That will be right after you finish *Curly Top*," he said.

"Will that be when you have your vacation, too, Daddy?" I wanted to know. You see, Daddy and Mom and I always go on our vacations together. It's nicest that way.

At first Mom wasn't so sure that I ought

"When you come back I'll teach you new dances,"
said Mr. Bill Robinson. He did. I do them
in my new picture, "The Littlest Rebel."

MY LIFE AND TIMES

to go on such a long trip. She was afraid I might get seasick. You feel awful bad when you're seasick, Corky. I mean I *think* you do. I didn't get seasick at all so I don't know. I said: "If I get sick, we can just turn around and come back." Then Mom laughed. "That's just the trouble, Presh. You can't turn the ship around and come back."

The captain wouldn't do it just for one little girl, don't you understand, Corky?

Well, finally we made up our minds to go. Oh, how busy we all were! Mom had to get dresses made. I had to go to the dentist to make sure that my teeth would last till we got back. Daddy had to see that we had enough trunks and bags and boxes for all our clothes.

I got so many presents in Honolulu—parasols, and fans, and slippers, and oh, so many things!

MY LIFE AND TIMES

Then I had to say good-bye to all my friends at the studio. When I met Mr. Bill Robinson, he said: "Now don't forget any of your dances, Shirley. And when you get back I'll teach you some new ones." He did. I do them in my newest picture *The Littlest Rebel.*

I went into the rabbit-hutch back of the bungalow and said good-bye to all my rabbits. They looked sad. I suppose they wanted to come along with me. It's too bad we didn't have enough room for them. Why, we could take only one of my dolls. We didn't even have enough room for you, Corky, and I like you best of all.

What a fine time I had on the ship! You've no idea how much water there was all around

MY LIFE AND TIMES

us. Every day we played games on the deck. I liked the game with the horses the most. Of course they weren't real horses. They were made of wood. The sailors pushed them from one place to another. They let me push them, too. You have to be pretty strong to push a horse.

One day I went up into the captain's office on the bridge. Only it wasn't the regular kind of bridge that goes across a river. They call it a bridge because that's the only name it's got. I helped steer the ship. Daddy called me "Cap'n Shirley" after that, and kept saluting me and saying, "Aye, aye, sir!" That's steamship language, and it means "Yes, sir."

The next day we came to Honolulu. At

MY LIFE AND TIMES

first it looked like a little bird sitting on the water at the end of the sky. Little by little it grew larger and greener. Then I saw trees, and the waves breaking on the white sand. And do you know, Corky, when we finally got close I saw something on the land that looked like flags and dresses and flowers and faces, all mixed up together. Do you know what it was? It was a great crowd of people. I thought something must be the matter.

"I guess there must be somebody on this boat they're waiting to see," Daddy said.

Goodness gracious, Corky, they were waiting to see me!

I know, because they all started shouting my name. I waved to them from the deck. When I got off the boat, they shouted more

MY LIFE AND TIMES

and more. They were all smiling. They certainly looked glad to see me. They all knew me all right. Only I didn't know *them*. It's hard to know what to say to your friends when you don't know them—and especially when there are so many of them.

Then we went to the Governor's palace. Oh, Corky, there were more friends waiting to say hello to me in front of the palace than there were at the dock! I could hear them shouting for me to come out even after we were inside the palace, talking to the Governor. This is what we decided to do. Mom and Daddy took my hands and we all went out on the balcony. All the people shouted "Hooray!" They wanted me to sing them a song. Mom whispered to me: "Sing

MY LIFE AND TIMES

'The Good Ship Lollypop,' darling. I know they'll like it."

I had to sing that song *four times*, Corky. That's how much they liked it!

I got so many presents in Honolulu, I almost didn't have enough arithmetic left to count them. There were Japanese and Chinese dolls with black hair, and Hawaiian dolls with grass dresses, and boxes of candy, and parasols in all the colors of the rainbow (though parasols haven't got anything to do with rain, you know), and fans, and surf boards, and slippers, and oh, so many other things. Duke Kahanomoku wrote his name on one of my surf boards for good luck because he's such a wonderful swimmer.

The naval officers in Honolulu took me out

I even learned how to do a real hula-hula on the beach at Waikiki!

to their battleship in the harbor. They gave me a white uniform to put on. Then they called me "Commodore Shirley." (A commodore and a captain are about the same thing, except that it takes a little longer to say commodore.) And I even learned how to do a real hula-hula on the beach at Waikiki!

But there was one very sad thing that happened when I was in Hawaii, Corky. Poor Mr. Will Rogers died, far away in Alaska. They phoned Mom about it, and I cried and cried. I did like Mr. Rogers so, and Mom says I'll never see him again.

The biggest surprise of the whole trip, though, was the present which the little children of Japan gave me. It was a doll as

The biggest surprise of the whole trip was the present the little children of Japan gave me, a doll as tall as a lady.

MY LIFE AND TIMES

tall as a real Japanese lady, with real black hair, and a wonderful silk kimono and a fan and wooden slippers. She was dressed just like a bride. I wouldn't give that doll away for anything, Corky, not even when I grow up.